# An Isolated Storm

**Poetry by Kaye Spivey**
**Second Edition**

I0158972

For permission requests, inquire at sksuncloud@hotmail.com

Cover art & design: Kaye Spivey

Second Edition, 2016
Manufactured in the United States of America

ISBN: 978-1-943798-02-5

# Table of Contents

Dedicated to life, family, and making the most of every passing storm.

# An Image of Cherry Blossoms

What would change your life? I guess,
is what I'm asking.

An image of *sakura*
on a hill over
everything once loved and lost,
forgotten in the thick air,
whispers through branches.
You could read that in *haiku*
and not be satisfied.

Some people reach out early
but I stand still, collecting
petals in wicker baskets,
becoming the memory,
the claim it happened at all—
a tree that came before me,
planted and bloomed.

Resentment runs through water veins
beneath sinking hills.
I only graze the surface
wearing knock-off silk—
one of us must give
to make it right.

We look so quiet,
like you are the snow
and I keep you from melting.

# Notion of Romance

Winter stalks in
cold
and heavy.
I like to think that I would kill for love,
but I would not.
I would be the warning story,
afternoon lark in the breeze.
We cannot control ourselves
more than the leaves control
when they change and flake.
We kill for simpler reasons.
When winter comes in
we burn the trees.

## Asymmetry

If you reach out with one hand
you are intangible.
Two hands,
you become a master inside your own skin.
Cold concrete
snorts like pixie stix,
because they never do know
what makes you coldest,
what leaves you stale, bitter,
until you tell them.
We are all either the mirror
or the image.
Salt stains on linoleum
lead you to believe that you are both.

# A Return

I could have written about
how the trees looked like icicles
in the sunlight,
how that light hit the very edges
of the snow where it clung to pine needles.
The slow sink of gold
through the dense ponderosas.
But it was us
walking along the ski path
in the freezing cold, noses bit in -5 degrees
that I remember.
Spending time
as the only ones in the forest.
We dropped off our snowshoes
and came back for them.

# Unlimited

It stopped snowing as soon as I got back.
It wasn't magic for Christmas.
I used up the magic in November
when I was belonging,
when I was becoming
more than the camped out version
of an awkward teen
with nothing to show for it,
whose failures were peeping through
a little more strongly.

In November, death escaped me,
loss escaped me,
friends were something being defined
for the first time ever
by how easy it was to stand in the rain,
by how getting lost was the best adventure;
something we might have never seen,
tea and trains and cows and green-green-green.

English speaking countries and the unity
of a language
without barriers, friendship in music,
in history, in literature and drinking,
learning value again:
the weight of a pound in your hand
versus sitting out in the cold
or walking nine miles to see
nothing.
I ate it up too fast;
belonging, and old things are catching me.
shadows, childhood,
stagnation.

I thought I'd be a poet and then I read Matthew Dickman.
I thought I'd fall in love
but then I didn't.

It seems like you can't say "I miss you"
enough.
It seems like you can't say "I'm sorry" enough,
and I'm too young for that,
and I've got so much more than that.
It made sense in November.
I knew who I needed to say "I love you" to,
even though I didn't send postcards.
It's wait-and-see again this year.
In November
seeing was unlimited.

## Trees of Autumn

Heavy as the winter closes
down on all that's left
the yellow birds drift
like a smile on the tragic
green and white
that opened all our eyes
to life that left
them staring blankly
left our wide eyes
ever gaping
at a sound that wasn't
wide enough to fit
between our ears and through
the splish and splash I see
the waters come alive
before they drain away
our souls
let the yellow birds go
flying off to golden lands where
sit the seraphim
ready to denounce the name
of God
in hell the fires haven't lost
their charm as heavy
winter closes in
I see it in the gentle eyes
of dawn that's never waking
never waking to the yellow bird
who's crying through
the storm.
Has heaven lost its name?
Its name?
Dear god!
The winter has no name.

# A short promise to a beatnik

I saw the best minds of your generation
become the best minds of mine,
and what do you know?
We're obsessed with zombies.

I'll see you after the apocalypse, Ginsberg.
I'll see you when the soil becomes rain.

# Collecting

Something gives
between the weight of the wind against the trees
and the rainwater that hasn't slipped
from green branches.
Something slides
from a drop on the nose
and the top of the head
past puddles
still collecting and wide
with the shift of silt.
Something could lie on damp ground.
Something could rise like the worms from the dirt—
give, with the chill that it is.

# In Ditches

I'm terrified of your cold hands,
the way they mock me,
the promises I can't expect them to keep.
I'm terrified of cattail reeds,
waving sadly in a ditch.

I don't want to stop here.
I don't ever want to stop, but
better lives than mine have tried
and they found nothing for it.
I'm afraid of what they'll say,
or how long it may linger.

Your cold hands—
ghosts along the threads that didn't take.
Cattail reeds, growing up in ditches
till they explode,
to spiny stems.

I'm scared of what they'll say,
when they'll say it.
Your cold hands
wandering through memories
and marsh beds.

## Decisions

She stuck her hand
through the fiber glass.
Baby, baby
I'm sorry.
Please don't run and tell your mommy.
Five more glasses then I drink champagne,
seven more slippers,
Do you know my name?

She stuck her hand through the fiber glass.
When the waves roll in, the ocean
is like diamonds
the way they glitter from afar,
the way I catch my breath
when the wind shifts—
close my eyes.

Baby, baby, I'm sorry
She stuck her hand through the fiber glass.
I run and show,
run and show,
backsplash talks of triumph
on whole wheat,
when you close the lid—don't tell me.
I'm five glasses gone,
seven slippers, fallen
ink splashes, lower case.
The ocean

and the rain in the sun carries
like car beams.
She stuck her hand
through the fiber glass.
She broke her fingers.
She stuck her hand—

Baby, I'm so sorry,

she said she called you mommy
and we all tipped glasses
and lolled,
something with rhythm,
pink slivers, flunked ethos.

She stuck her hand out
and she caught it,
great big gobs
oozed slowly through her fingers
the way sand falls
at the base of the tide.
The way sand knows
to retreat.
Faded murmurs in the careless crowd.

Baby, baby, I'm sorry,
baby, I'm sorry, I'm sorry,

I'm sorry.

She left a shoe behind
like Cinderella.
She left a worn eraser
and a glass of chardonnay.

## Anxious

Think of it like a heartbeat,
somebody else's—
a rhythm ingrained in the patterns
of your speech,
that you only notice
when you're lying awake at night
and that throb
is pulsating through your neck
and temples—
something that should be so holy
you lie awake praying to it.
You lie awake thinking about what it means
to have a beating heart,
to be part of a system
that wants so desperately not to break.
To be the butterfly effect in a life
you haven't mastered,
to be scared with every heartbeat,
to lean heavily against the door frame
knowing his heart is beating too,
it's just not the same rhythm,
it's just not the same speed.

# A Letter From a Child

I lived in a state of other people's dreams
and burned myself on the arid vents.
I buried into the side of a mountain
and sought refuge
where clouds are infinite.

Do most people fall apart at 23
and make plans for 25?
Which will come just as quickly as tomorrow
and smell of ground coffee
never aerated from your clothes
because these things stay beneath your skin,
once they're there, they're permanent.
You choose them while you're young
and hope they'll match the you
on a shining stage of 57.

A you that napped in the wild flowers today
and didn't get groceries,
a you who stuck around for the snow to come
and grew strong shoveling the car out,
a you who made plans for 25,
and then for 35
and maybe kept them.
A you who is maybe successful
and maybe alone,
but did learn to dance with a boy
who asked you to keep writing,
who did find a place you call home,
and maybe is still happy.

In a world full of people going crazy,
I sit inside my eggshell.
Tonight
the moon is watching me.

## Cigarette

There's a cigarette still burning
in your limp hand.
The ashes begin to taint the carpet,
the smoke has started
to eat away at your lungs.
There's a part of me that wants
to get to know you again.
There's a part of me
that never missed it.

# On a Ship to Nowhere

Disrupt the silence, darling,
do you see where it leads?
This vessel only sails
through fog, through
the darkest nights.

A voice like yours,
it deserves the light.
Eyes like yours
crave a sight of day.

As long as you don't
blind yourself
on the glaring sun,
or grow harsh,
from the noise of the world,
it would be good for you
to leave this place.

You've always been too sweet
to sail on my ship
to dark and sheltered days.
The silence does nothing for you,
the air doesn't suit your needs.

Break into the light now, darling,
because from here
the fog invades your vision,
the night smothers every prayer.

## A Ride on the Bus

I catch the last lift.
Nothing else but silence and cars
will pass here again tonight.
I will be standing for the first half,
disinclined to accept a gentleman's invitation
to take his seat,
until we get to the station
and half the bus empties anyway.
Standing up, you feel the rocky tar
shake the bus side to side like a dingy
settled out upon the waves of some sputtering sea.
Seated, you're just another body,
swaying with the boat
as the current moves you on.
I hold my purse and watch the buildings pass
again and again in a rhythm of lights
until we slide into my stop.
I shuffle out with the crowd
and look about in wonder,
as if I didn't know exactly where I'd arrived.
I disregard the other commuters, who ignore me
as they stride off with purpose
back to their computers and TV screens.
I stretch against the jarring of my back
where the vigorous rocking of the bus
has set it out of line.
It's nearly midnight but even way out here
I still can't see the stars.
I miss the clear night skies,
when the moon's the only light
and the sky goes on forever,
like it is young again.

# Cure

Use bitter leaves
they say
to cure the cold
that leaks beneath the window frame.
Use bitter leaves
to shake out all the pain.
Crush them and drink out the oils
that kept them green and new;
they'll warm the deepest cold.
Use bitter leaves
they say
it's the only cure you haven't tried.
Use bitter leaves
because the fruit's sweet nectar
only left you ailing.

## Flurries

I stand by crystal light tapping,
or typing on the frozen glass,
messages of want, or waiting
the kind which I should be
too young to understand.

I don't want to wake the room,
only to softly strike the keys
of every little mocking bird
landing just beyond the pane.
If I can tap upon the glass just right
the tiny birds will align
through the vibrations
and become the words I can't say,

but in the quiet of the room,
no one will see them.
White upon white
they fade away.

# Lights Down the Alleyway

How can something so cold be burning?
be turning back on itself
in the light nudge
it gives to wanderers,
to unsteady feet
slipping into mud,
running to catch the last flicker,
the glow of the bulbs
before
and behind,
barely lighting the way.
Soaked socks over soaked toes,
dreading how beautiful
the first snow will be
when it falls, catching in the light.
At the end of the alley a bulb bursts
and it is warm again.

## Standard Visibility

Do you see me?
I am a crowded space.
The No Vacancy sign above my head
is lit.
A certain kind of capacity has been met—

but feel free to try to sneak in the back door,
past my heart.
It doesn't care.
It's smoking in the alley.
It will go home early tonight.

# Catharsis

If you want to
you can pick up and go at anytime,
anywhere you want.
How many times have I said that?
Still, so many chapters
wind up trashed in revision.

I want to see you,
isn't that a legitimate thought?
Isn't crushing you into a sticky sap of mulch
a legitimate thought?

If I rewrite letters,
if I arrange texts
and song lyrics,
if I lie awake at night and learn *Nihongo*,
if one week I'm in Los Angeles
and the next I hit the coast
fleeing for clean air and soft lights,
if I'm crying one moment out of fear
and the next for sadness
and then I'm laughing—

We're sharing apple cider out of teacups
and the sea breeze is cold
somewhere,
next year.

If what we amount to is the number of cats
we save from heatstroke and strangers,
if almond milk is the glue
for lives torn apart,
if you can remove yourself from one moment
and land casually in the next
as though nothing ever happened,
lose six rounds to the treadmill
and one staring at the bathroom ceiling

listening to music you can't translate.

If you miss every shifting rhythm,
every mistake,
every subtle glance
because maybe no one cares—

If you wanted, you could be anywhere by tomorrow.
If you wanted, I'd go with you.
We could leave by yesterday
get there before this morning,
before last night,
before three years passed
and the house got too heavy to live in,
too full to leave.

# There Are No Ghosts Here

There is a life song
that comes in a phrase of moans.
Last night I dreamt I saw a ghost,
just the feet
moving toward me.
Tonight I will wait up
and go to work in a fit of exhaustion.
I will write a poem
for the you I live with
and drink tea and the sunshine
over mountains
all winter.

The moans of the house
when the wind blows,
I will wear them
triple layer.
I will leave the poem on the counter
and lock the door when I leave.
Tonight
I will dream of holocausts and wake up
and sleep again.

The you is never present,
always a tip
to a memory or a promise,
always
a cyclical romance
slipping like the sheets
off the bed
when I don't go back to sleep.
I know I am alone
and I listen.

## Summer

Dreams get caught up,
too big for mason jars
full of fireflies
aglow in late august,
too deep for wishing wells
when a penny's too steep,
floating in the black spaces
between anxiety and regret
and something you wish you could see in the sunset,
casting off toward wonder that sparks
while three of those fireflies blink a quiet S.O.S.
over a cup of spiced tea
you pay attention to the storm rolling in over the mountains,
not the rose bush that sprang up by the wall,
or the thistle towers, and chokecherry
cascading into the apple trees,
the cool scent of something
you almost—just barely remember.
A summertime
too short for dreams.

# A Quiet Melody Calls You

*Based on ideas in Ai Yazawa's 'Kagen no Tsuki'*

That's not the right path through the gate,
up the stairs into the old house.

If you don't follow me you could get lost.
Stop and listen. Don't let me lose you.

There's water damage pooling on the floor,
but the piano still plays

in the room upstairs, three keys missing,
strings rusted and snapped.

It's a clear, soft melody,
written to keep someone here,

To lure them back from the gate.
I can take you to safety. I can be the thread

tied to your finger. I'll show you the path.
Mind the broken boards. Mind the shattered glass.

The piano still plays
a familiar song, slow and bright.

The last quarter moon slips in
through rat holes and missing shingles,

illuminating a broken guitar, missing the E strings.
The song becomes a duet.

You'll be lost if you don't trust me.
Take my hand—the lights fade out behind you.

I will guide you where the moonlight is brighter,
where there is wind upon your face again.

# Dreamcatcher

You use wishes for wishes,
that's what they're meant for.

You close your eyes tight
and breathe,

locks of wind
carry courage to your cheeks.

*Daijoubu desu ka? (Are you okay?)*
*Tsukareta? (Are you tired?)*

You don't use charms,
rocks, or legends,

you don't catch dreams.
You lock slivers of wind in your hair,

you carry them with you,
the lucid part of a memory.

Leave the stars in the sky,
leave luck to empty space.

You use wishes and save pennies,
carry them in a jar marked "Yesterday."

*Daijoubudarou? (Will you be okay?)*
*Ashita desu ne? (Isn't it tomorrow?)*

# Shipwreck

Some people come in smooth,
sails blown taut in the wind,
but you tripped up the rocks
and lay beaten beside the lighthouse door.

What makes some of us so drawn to the light,
siren's beam from the crags,
when others can avoid it
and dock safely in the port?

You came to a wreck.
What did you learn from that?

The light circles above your head.
You can just watch it blink
round and round in certainty forever,

or you can stumble back here.
I have watched you from the shore,
debris floats toward me and banks
at my feet.

You can trip back from the light,
I'll meet you halfway in a rowboat.
I'll bring a blanket.
I'll pull you in
before the sea.

## In Meter

The air is not so warm as night sets in.
That lick of coolness calms my fevered cheek.
A storm may be rolling in from somewhere
West of here, where the oceans hoard the rain.
I should be wrapped inside, drinking tea,
warding off whatever plagues my spirit.
Yet this clean air will do more to cure me
than that hot, stuffy room and all those pills.
I come alive for the first time in days
Watching the stars come out and kiss my eyes
and bring me back to what health really is.

## Monsoons

The rain changes everything a little bit,
redirects the morning,
the spitfire breath

of nine hour days lazes off
to the lightning and thunder
that doesn't scare anyone

when it cracks across the whole, wide sky
and leaves footprints of the storm
in the corners of the clouds.

A moment for a coffee break,
a moment for sometimes we stand around waiting
as the warm air rises off the mountains

and the clouds sink down,
fill in the spaces
where the sea used to be.

## Signals

You and I have only drifted into
this hall to escape
the cold, the rain.
We're seeking shelter, perspective,
words too close to penetrate,
too alive to get lost
in still air. You and I are

young, younger than we imagine.
I have come in without a voice,
and I may go before it's found,
but right now you're so close,
even in silence there are things
you have to say, whether or not
I hear them, whether or not

we've drifted out again,
or the room records
our words and projects them
into the cold, damp night,
so that all the world is silent
for just one moment, and you
and I are so close, almost touching,
lost among fractured voices
drifting in and out of dim light.

# Racing

I'm tired of this track;
the speed set by the lead car
whipping around and around
but going nowhere we haven't been
a hundred, two hundred times.
I'm ready to drive on a straight road,
one with a horizon and destination
and no more terror that I
might swerve and crash into you
or you into me in our secret goal
to come in second;
because no one really intends to usurp the lead.

I want to pass by houses, dark or lit,
and fields of wheat or corn,
and miles of yellow prairie grass
past life after life,
instead of endless steel seats
and the same lights flashing;
left around this corner, left around that one.

I hate feeling ashamed
if I take my foot off the gas and bow out,
losing my place as everyone races
ahead, because you can't admit
when you have to stop
on this track.
It's not like the straight, Midwestern highways
where I could slug along for hours
and only the occasional semi would honk,
passing me by in its hurry to be somewhere,
possibly the same place I'm headed
just a few hours behind;
some dust-ripped prairie town
with twenty porch lights
and one motel.

# The Damages

Left alone and stranded I have felt
the bottom of the damages.
I have felt the shallowness

of my situation,
blockaded around words
of secret poverty

and secret gain.
Life lets lessons lay discarded
to be picked up and sorted

by the stragglers
with extra time to burn
in the same fires that burned books;

a useless show of too much self-importance,
because we can always write more
if we find the courage,

we can always drag ourselves—
face first—to our knees—straightened legs—
hair pulls back once it's long enough,

once it's found time to grow.
Respite strikes
the nonbelievers too.

# A Heart so Wild

It's like you'd been inside
that space I couldn't slide into,

I, the quiet storm
still out of step
and tumbling up the coast.

You reminded me that trees grew here,
and that when they were restless
they picked up
and sailed.

You reminded me of what the wind can do
when you stop standing in it
and let it move you.

# Eyes

You could be my muse—
the magic of the night,
shifting away into stars
and dim lit places even strays don't venture,
cold latte spilled on sidewalks,
long dried up
into an image you'll find in a museum someday,
if that artist ever finds a stage
and if the music's amped out into the night,
who knows what kind of story that will be?
Something you'd stay up for,
just to trip that moment
on repeat—
red lines and a clean verse,
stars fill up my vision
and sink into the lights.

# Sunshowers

A singular event—
a fox wedding rain,
where the sun shines through
and the drizzle
just barely kisses
the curve of the leaves.
If you had a choice you would pause here.
If you had a choice,
you would run wildly.

## If This Night's Forever

If this night is forever,
I won't let it down.
I'll spend it seeking a god
and looking for mercenaries,
or escape in a mad dash to the gate.
I'll jump countries in the night
before you'll ever know I've left,
and I'll turn down the sheets early
so we'll both believe I've gone to bed.
I'll learn French and drink teas
that didn't have a name before England.
I'll build a sailboat and scale
high walls in search of grape vines
and vast fields of tulips and roses
growing just out of reach of the sea.
I'll read through novels and be brilliant
and wash my feet in seashells
until I'm beautiful and clean.
I'll write songs for a lover
and letters to lost friends and invent
a way to Tango that doesn't include our feet.
I'll sit until sunrise in a coffee bar,
drinking latte after latte and making small talk
and paper cranes from napkins,
waiting for the sun to get carried away.
So that by the time you know I'm gone
I'll have forgotten all the little threads
that wove me here in the first place,
or be hard at work making a quilt of them.

# About the Author

Kaye Spivey is a writer who lives in the Pacific Northwest with her boyfriend and two cats, Pi and Mulan. She loves poetry, tea, and stormy weather and writes or reads whenever she isn't playing video games. Her roaming lifestyle has inspired much of her poetry and helped shaped her appreciation of close friends and family. Spivey has had poetry previously published in such literary journals as Written River, Sterling Mag, Ghostlight, The Penwood Review, and Northwest Boulevard, among others. This is her first poetry chapbook.

# Acknowledgements

*"A Heart so Wild"* and *"Monsoons"* previously appeared in Volume 4, Issue 2 of Written River

*"If This Night's Forever"* and *"A Short Promise to a Beatnik"* previously appeared in the fall 2012 edition of Sterling Magazine

*"Unlimited"* previously appeared in the 2012 edition of Northwest Boulevard

*"Catharsis"* and *"Standard Visibility"* previously appeared in the 2014 edition of Northwest Boulevard

*"A Ride on the Bus"* was a finalist in the 2010 Poetry Ark contest

*"Trees of Autumn"* previously appeared in the 2009 second edition of Skyline Review

*"On a Ship to Nowhere"* previously published in Volume 2, Issue 1 of Ghostlight

*"Cure"* published August 2009 on www.thirtyfirstbird.com

www.ingramcontent.com/pod-product-compliance
Lightning Source LLC
Chambersburg PA
CBHW020441030426
42337CB00014B/1342